the orchid

the orchid

the northern collection II

k. tolnoe

when the spring comes
and everyone unfolds
you feel stuck
like layers and layers of your potential
your thoughts and musings
are folded and tucked away
in your core
only waiting to find a way out
but it seems like
you don't sprout and grow
as easily as others
who have always known their way
but your wavering flower heart
and your observant nature
is not a flaw
it's your greatest strength
for your fine sense of belonging
your soft heart and kind hands
will take you home
to where you truly belong
and when you finally learn to listen
to find the right surroundings
you will thrive and bloom
to discover
that you were always
the orchid

empathy is a heavy gift

my skin is not thin
it's non-existent
my environment is not around me
but within me
there is no line between my soul
and the outside world
every emotion that flows
with the touches and the winds
settles down within
and i carry them around
wondering
if i'm the only one burned
by the intensity of the colors
in other people's eyes
if i'm the only one fighting
for every breath
due to the bonds
that are tied around my chest
with the words of every story
i have ever heard
i am not one person in the world
i am the world in one person
and sometimes the burdens
of the human race
is all that i am

like butterflies
people only stay for a while

you are the only one
rooted in your life
everyone else has wings
that will bring them to you
and take them away again
like any flower
we need their love and help
to grow. to bloom. to reproduce
but we must also remember
nothing is promised
and we all reach a point
where we can do nothing more
for each other
eventually history unfolds in a way
that forces wings in the air
it's the turn of time
the law of nature
and there is nothing we can do
except to let them go

save some love for yourself

your heart is a fountain
fresh drops of mineral love
fall from your fingers
when you reach out to touch
dry skin
you water everyone around you
and they sprout like a garden
but somehow you have gotten
so used to their enchanting colors
that you find no rainbow
in the mirror
you smile at everyone
except your reflection
you're so caught up
in the drought of this world
that you no longer feel
your own thirst
but even your softness has limits
your heart could run dry
if you do not realize
that you too
are a flower
deserving of everything
you usually give away

every unhealed wound is another thorn

the pain is part of the pact
of energy
that we usually call life
humans are a combination
of tough minds and tender skin
running through a world
full of holes and thorns
some wounds are nothing
but a light scratch
some betrayals are broken bones
that grow together in wrong ways
sharp as thorns
if we do not tend to them
it feels as if
we will never be the same again
in the mirror we see
a brand new face
with drowned eyes and sharp lines
so we learn to protect ourselves
with poison words and hard hands
but that itself
is a tragedy
for when you shut out the pain
you also turn off
every chance of true happiness

a good heart is not always a good thing

we praise kindness and love
but maybe there's such a thing
as giving too much
for your mind is a garden
your heart a beating bud
a soft home
ready to unfold in love
and flowers grow from your wrists
when you invite someone in
the problem is that
not everyone who enters
is there to admire
but to acquire
that's why cats have claws
and why roses grow thorns
because sad as it is
we live in a world
where love does not equal love

take notes on life
no lesson is worth learning twice

things happen
and people come and go
all with the purpose
of teaching you something new
and whatever you learn
recognize the lessons
and remember them
when you move on
for if you don't
you'll be forced to make
the same mistakes
again and again
until you either crush
under the weight of them
or finally come
to understand
that there's always a reason
for things to happen
in a certain way

the orchid

every petal must eventually fall

every rise from the ground
will eventually turn into a fall
and every flower is destined
to wither away
even those with a beating heart
and a human breath
time will take everything
away from us
even ourselves
so while you hold the
moments in your hand
may you remember to look up
as well as within
and enjoy the fireworks
of color and form
that makes spring
the most memorable season of all
before the clocks turn
and it's all gone again

the orchid

love is not supposed to make you feel like that
it's all him

do not lose your faith in love
but in him
for what he is giving you
is a paper heart
that crumbles with time
the softness you expected
is replaced with sharp edges
cutting open your mind
draning you of energy and hopes
and giving nothing but
emptiness
back
it may be a fire
but it will never keep you warm
all you get is the smoke
clouding your mind
and clocking your throat
no matter how much you want
it to work
you cannot deny that it hurts
it is a poor imitation
of the gold you deserve
of what is out there
waiting for you

he asked me
"did you hope for more?"
and i said
"i always do"

i am not naturally lightweight
my soul is old
heavy with thousands of years
and so i do not thrive
naturally
i feel the fear. the pain. the guilt and the grief
sometimes more than i feel
the hope
i try to walk lightly
but more often than not
the ground under my feet breaks
under the weight of my sorrows
i keep falling down
into the hole of my own mind
and that's the thing about being deep
when you reach the bottom
of your soul
there is no light at all
and in those moments
it becomes hard to breathe
but it explains
how others have a hard time
taking care of my needs
accepting and loving me
when i cannot do it myself

i am homesick for myself

there was a time
when i was known for my strength
for so long i knew exactly
where i wanted to be
and how to get there
but somewhere along the way
my heart changed
i saw a path
that i never could have imagined
and now i'm lost between two worlds
desperately in need
of faith
for i hold all the answers
somewhere between my hands
and my head
all i want to know
is how to change
back into myself

caring can be a curse

i am blessed to bloom
and cursed to wither away
for i always care
and my feelings flower fast
even in the most barren of grounds
where nothing else will grow
i tend to plant gardens
where nobody wants them
i give them both my rain
and my sun
all that i am
and that is a shame
for over and over again
am i forced to watch
the love i have to give
and the connection i wish to share
as it dies
and fall to the ground as waste
in the gap
between lovers and friends

they mistake your softness
for weakness
but there is so much power
in forgiving rather than revenging
in whispering rather than yelling
in spreading your wings to fly
rather than staying to fight
when they light a spark
for fire cannot be killed by flames
only by the slow ocean waves
that are your grace

but tell me
love
how much can your smile carry?

the orchid

there is hope in everything
even pain

the world may not be kind
or even fair
but it is so full of life
that everything is possible
even peace
for everything with the ability
to breathe
has the power to change
even a bleading heart can heal
even a dead flower
has a chance to bloom again
for as long as we have ourselves
nothing is truly the end
not even that kind of pain
that turns the sun dark
nothing is more powerful than time
and even if you will never be
the same person again
you still have a possibility
to be truly great
so this is the truth
i choose to hold on to
the seasons may change
but the hope always remains

the fear of feeling is fear of living

our emotions are both the chains
and the breaker of them
for the art is in the contrast
the fresh thrill of the mountain top
as well as the crushing despair
of the ocean floor
we were sat in this diverse world
for a reason
to explore it all
it has so much to offer
there's a place in every person
and adventure in every location
your inner world is a reflection
of all the life around you
all waiting to be opened up
explored and touched
but if you refuse
to accept the darker parts
if you're too scared of the fall
to ever take the first step
the point of this story will remain
an unresolved mystery

the orchid

some mistakes are miracles

sometimes it seems
as if this life
is a house of cards
and with one wrong move
it all comes crashing down
burying you in the darkness
of heavy emotions
but this does not mean
you have to die
no
this is your chance
to finally come alive
to sprout and to grow
from what was meant to destroy you
for all glorious lights things
come from the darkest of places

yesterday has nothing for us

this life is a lesson
in release
with every moment that passes
we must let go
of what was
every day that goes by
means we're losing time
and it's terrifying
so we try to hold on
by looking back
and remembering it all
but while the past
may be filled with love
laughter and good memories
it holds no new opportunities
the future may be painted
with worry and anxiety
but it's also the home of hope
of possibility
all it need
is our energy

those who couldn't return your love
needed it the most

k.tolnoe

i squeezed rain from the clouds
stole light from the stars
cut my hands on their edges
and let the blood flood
to color your petals
i covered the frozen ground with my hands
to turn the soil moist and warm
all to see you thrive
you grew a body full of flowers
but you chose
to keep them to yourself
all that i gave
was never given back to me
still my love brought more lushness
to this world
that often seems such a barren place
and that i believe
is never a waste

i am a scale
with a soul that craves balance
harmony and stillness
in a world
that never stops spinning
i am constantly torn
by different parts of myself
the highest artist
and the lowest human being
caught in the crossfire
between wishes and dreams
and fears and logic
running after one thing
but being pulled by another
what i want is right there
in the middle line of it all
yet i cannot hold on
even though it's only
one simple thing
i tend to speak as if
all i want to do is leave
but in truth what i pray for
in the night
is peace

as a giver you must know your worth
the takers won't tell you

nothing is rarer
than a genuine wish
to give more than you take
we are the flowers
the butterflies and the stars
of this world
enduring a lifelong process of pain
of breaking, dissolving and burning
to bring a little more beauty
and hope into the world
nothing is more precious
than the gold in your bones
so do not let anyone
take it away from you
do not get caught up in their cages and chains
of tight words
never let anyone tell you
what you're worth
and put your freedom
before anything
for doubt grows easily
in a mind of sensitivity
and this world needs you
more than you need it

maybe this love will find a home
in another time

this thing between us
our shared soul
is light and soft like bubbles
it drifts around with the wind
covering us in a silky shine
that paints the world in pink and white
our mistake is that
we try to catch it
to make it stay
we hold on so tightly
because we want it so badly
and then we break it
with our violent touch
so maybe this time we try
to let it be
and even let it leave
for if it is truly art
it will come back
when the frame is right

ground in yourself first

you are a creature of love
on the move
searching for hearts
in which to root yourself
but the thing about humanity
is that it's both wild and free
we cannot always control
where we stay
and when we leave
i see it in your eyes
feel it in the hesitation
of your hands when you reach out
you have loved so many times
only to see your trust cut
when they moved on
so before you attach yourself
to another falling star
reach into yourself
let your roots start
in your own eternal light
and the world will never
go dark

if you have the ability
to imagine a better world
you also have the power
to create it

i saw the crushed light
in his eyes
and mistook it for stars
i felt the heavy burdens
on her shoulder blades
and called them wings
i found all these wild colors
spilling from my mind
my mouth and my eyes
and caught them with my hands
i painthed them across the ceiling
and called it a rainbow
maybe that's my greatest flaw
but also what creates the art
the ability to find
the most enchanting beauty
in what's broken

the orchid

all growth takes time

when it comes to growth
your patience is your power
for unfolding takes time
whether you're a human
or a flower
i know you've been holding back
for so long
and now that you've found
your roots
you cannot wait
to touch the clouds
but growth is a process
and while grass grows fast
it's easily broken
but the oak tree
which takes years and year to complete
will not fear any storm
for it will always stand tall and strong
so darling
don't forget
that steady and slow
is the best way to grow

the orchid

turn your head into your home

your mind is the frame
of the art
that is your life
there is no way out of it
no way to escape
without hurting yourself
so make it comfortable
make it your own
build it on your dreams
furnish with your ideas
and decorate it
with your wishes
invite your favorite guests
and let go of everyone
who cannot behave
for when your own head
becomes your home
you can go wherever
with whomever
and never feel alone

the orchid

we all start with nothing
being born naked and alone
with nothing to hold on to
but the belief and the hope
that we can become something more
but this world is both heavy
and cold
it will bury us
under the weight
of a life of pain and sorrow
it will try and hold us down
with tiny frames and hard structures
to keep our wild side inside us
until we lose track
of our own values
and lose our true calling
in a life
someone else created for us

but no matter what happens
and how much time passes
no lies can kill
the truth of our nature
deep within us
we all have the potential
to become anything
and everything at once
we are the culmination of evolution
and design
and when it's combined
with a lust for this life
we find the power to rise
to touch the sky
and lift others with us
for turning into the greatest and most vibrant
of our kind
is what we are all here for

your love is a mirror

no matter where you're looking
into whose eyes you're gazing
you will only see
your own love reflected
for that's the thing about affection
it may end between us
but it starts inside us
there is no real connection
to another human being
if your heart is separated
from your mind
so remember that
whatever you're seeing
is a reflection of yourself
and the more you give
the more you become
the more you care
the more you'll be loved

an ending is not the end

flowers bloom to wither
the sun rise to set
and we were all
born to die
everything changes
and like a butterfly
what we come to love
will eventually escape from us
but this is no reason
to kill the flowers
that grow from your chest
to let go of the hope
that this life is worth it
that we could become whole
for no amount of endings
will end the new beginnings
more colors and new life
will come with the next season
and who knows
maybe the best of it all
is still waiting for us

the orchid

only fake flowers are flawless

you may not be in full fresh bloom
all the time
you may not be
the best version of yourself
every day
but darling
who could be?
changing with the seasons
falling with the drought
rising with the flood
is all part of being real
of being alive
you are in sync
with every living creature
spinning with the world
and breathing with the earth
if you want to be perfect
you have to be in plastic

healing is about accepting
not forgetting

those moments
where everything changes
have a tendency to burn
themselves in our brains
how could i forget
the tearful eyes
of every early goodbye
the cold spots
on my skin and in my sheets
where the love used to be
but the point is not to erase
every memory
that ever brought you pain
but to accept them
to let them live
in your body
and to realize
that sometimes only the wrong situations
will send you the right way

the orchid

you will never grow
if you have to mourn every leaf
that falls

it is a rule as old
as our world
before the moon comes out
the sun must go down
the caterpillar must be completely gone
for the butterfly to unfold
the trees must shed their leaves
in order for new to sprout
and sometimes cutting yourself down
taking a step back
is the only way
to move forward
for in order to make space
for the new to come
you must let go of the old
and the more you accept it
the faster you grow

live your story
before it's over

it is tempting
to wait for life to happen
to push the happiness in front of us
expecting it to live in another time
for it keeps the hope alive
but this is the story
not the prologue
do not lose today
in the idea of tomorrow
for every moment wasted
is eternally lost
and the time we spend
regretting and worrying
about the future and the past
is not coming back
so savor every moment
anchor yourself in the present
and write a magnificent tale
or else your story
may not start
before it ends

family is made with bonds
not blood

we all need a place
to call home
somewhere to be held and loved
somewhere to belong
but this place is not always
where we were born
for family is so much more
than just shared blood
it can be found all around the world
if you're lucky enough
in the end it doesn't matter
who shares your genes
or carry your name
it matters who holds you
who supports you
who welcomes you home
even when you've been gone
for too long
family is when you share a bond
with someone
strong enough to set them free
and always welcome them back again

take time to kiss yourself

your skin is hugging tight
around your bones
taking on a hue
of cold indigo blue
for when you try to escape your past mistakes
you're erasing the lines of your own figure
turning into a ghost
in an attempt
to never get in your own way
you feel strangled within yourself
begging for someone
to offer an easy escape
out of your own head
but your waiting is useless
and it will go on forever
for the healing power
the forgiving flower words
the younger you is asking for
could never come from someone else
it must come from your own lips
when you let their watery warmth
touch your own skin
and whisper
you are okay

a late bloom is still beautiful

just as all the flowers
cannot bloom at the same time
you should never think of yourself
as further ahead
as farther behind
for we are moving at our own pace
and going to a unique place
so there is no need to rush
for the universe is moving in circles
and it works in second chances
it doesn't know
what is early and what is late
it only shows
when the time is right

every emotion has a story to tell

our emotions are both visitors
and messengers
they tell stories
of who we once were
and the things that happened
even those we can't remember
they bear witness
of the loves we once held
that left and came back
with new names
for everything we feel
is rooted in ourselves
not our surroundings
so if you want to leave
if you want to change
don't run away
from your own story
start to listen

you were a deep brilliant blue
in my world of soft pastels

all i want to do
is dance slow in the moonlight
with a flower crown in my hair
and chains of rain around my wrists
another hand in mine
a liquid flame of passion
running over my skin
moving with the music
and the wavy grass under my feet
it's all i wish for
details of softness
that let us exist
in a world
that finally matches
my soul

may you find peace
within your pain

this is what the lotus does
from the darkest of places
a grave of mud
it rises
with every open wound
unfolding as a petal
even despite all of the darkness
it has known
it refuses to die
it remains open
and this is my hope for you
that somehow and sometime
you may find the courage within
to do the same
to see that everything that happened to you
brought you to yourself
that all the light you're wishing for
is coming your way
that you may finally come to rest
in the pain
of your past

everything will come together
in the right time

the universe is the greatest creator
nature the most complex masterpiece
for everything is so carefully designed
that it all work together
for a higher power
even the disasters and the flaws
the foundation of the wild
is the balance between opposites
and so everything happens in a way
that maintan the greater picture
the thing is
as humans we only see a tiny part
we are a single stroke
on the painting of life
constantly wondering
which purpose we have
without realizing
only time will show
how it was all connected
from the very beginning

kindness always comes back

kindness is selfish
it is something you do for yourself
for when you find the courage and strength
to smile at a stranger
in a time of pain
you're sending a gift with time
to your future self
when you give others a hand
even when your whole body
is trembling with weight
and you help them
rebuild what was broken
while your own pieces
are still cutting you open
know that
it will be remembered
and when you feel the most lost
a guiding light
of your own kindness
will find its way
back to you

honor your heart

there is no finer guide
no kinder light
or no more loyal friend
than the beating spirit
in your chest
fighting to keep you alive
every minute of every day
lighting up your life
with passion and strives
and it even has its own wishes
dreams and desires
but it is soft and shy
so easily blocked by the mind
and the rush of our daily life
so don't forget to honor it
by taking time
to be quiet
to listen to its slow song
and adjust your rhythm
to the beating of your heart
for that is the only way
to align who you want to be
with who you are

nothing is too small
to make a difference

as humans
we try so hard to see the bigger picture
that we forget to see the tiny pieces
that make the greatest difference
everything is connected
and even the most complicated systems
are depending on the details
in a world
where something as small
as a bacteria
can break the balance
of an empire
or put everything back
in its rightful place
you may sometimes fell small
weak and powerless
but don't you ever dare to think
that it makes you irrelevant

some feelings never leave

art is timeless
in the way it stays relevant
and binds hearts
across generations
the way a stroke of paint
imitates the secret images
hidden on the inside
of our eyelids
or how a story
crawls through our veins
word by words
until it reaches our chest
and stop the beating with an ending
we've heard before
it explains
how some losses and loves
tend to stay with us
in their freshest shapes
how some memories
cannot be dulled or erased
for if it's important enough
to be kept in a human heart
time holds no power

stay wherever you find hope

the darkness is always nearby
attempting to make a home
out of your eyes
so if there is a place
that lights a fire in your mind
that sends the shadows on a flight
and warms up the blood in your veins
so you can shape the world
with your bare hands
if there is a person
that makes you want to
get up and try again
even if the odds are against
your very existence
stay there
and never let go
for hope is the sunlight
we all need to grow

the earth is your canvas

what a magnificent gift
to live in a world of breathing art
where every tiny movement
becomes part of the greatest story
ever told
our bodies are paintbrushes
and our thoughts the colors
the ideas and dreams
come together in complex motives
that we bring to life
with the touch of a hand
for the world is a blank canvas
waiting for us
to let our passion guide us
and create a masterpiece
where we are both
the artists
and the art itself

i often dream of replacing my heart
with a rose
full of its blooming beauty
soft to every loving touch
but not as unable to protect itself
from those only seeking
to possess

this is the power of new beginnings
the charm of the morning sun
the allure of spring

the belief
that you can become anything

you are nothing
but light

there are no limits
to your influence
you are soft and indomitable
like the morning light
you neither ask or apologize
when you change worlds
with a kind touch
you just are
and you cannot be contained
or defined
not in numbers
in words or in shapes
for when your body dies
you are the part
that squirms out of your shell
like a snake sheds it skin
and you return
to the the stars
and the salty ocean waves
to bring hope to them
still held by the darkness

sometimes the right place is a person

it seems like
we are all searching
for where we belong
a place to call home
but i've traveled the world
and i never found any solid ground
that holds me as well
as your hand
i never saw an ocean
that carries me as well
as your mind
and this is when i realized
home is about connection
the feeling of being softly held
and sometimes you can only find that
in a person
not a place

the orchid

the spring always comes

everything moves in circles
even time
the years is a wheel
that keeps spinning around
and even when the winter
feels like the ending
know that warmer days are coming
the sun is the only thing
we can truly trust
to always come back to us
the hope. the light. the warmth
it will always find its way
and melt the frost away
even in the core of the forest
even in the coldest of souls
no matter where you are
the new beginning will come
even in places
it has never been before

your heart knows your truth

we all have our own truths
on who to be
and where to go
but this world is filled with noise
voices drowning your thoughts out
until your mind is hazy
with smoke of doubt
if this year
was a lesson in listening
may the next be the time
of bravery and courage
where i remember to hear that voice
follow its words
and forget to apologize for it
for no one
not even those i love
could ever guide me
as precisely as my heart

oh but little bee
the spring is here
so why are you not spreading
your wings?
the fear is in you
not around you
everything else is ready
and you were built for this movement
every line in your body
point in this direction
the ground is calling you home
putting pressure on you
but you were created to defy it
your mind is in the air
and it's time you join it there
my tiny love
what are you so afraid of?
if you dare to open your eyes
and look around
you will see
all the flowers
are blooming for you

i dream with my eyes wide open

my mind knows no difference
between day and night
the stars shimmer constantly
in the edges of my vision
even when i close my eyes
i see sun rays dancing
with every color of the sky
my dreams are not linked
to my bed
the fairytales are not locked
away in the books
they make a home
out of my head
and i see them everywhere
in strangers' eyes
in the electric air between our hands
and in the lines of light
when we start to dance
no matter where i look
i see the magic
because i know
that it exists

i spent the beginning of my life
thinking i was the only one of my kind
until i met you
and you opened your heart
without me having to ask
i recognized myself in your eyes
heard an echo of my own story
in your words
but i would have never known
if you had not unfolded
into my art
this connection has inspired me
to embrace
every part of this sensitive being
the heavy soul
and the light words
thank you for carrying it all
with me

-to my reader

acknowledgements

to my mother
for caring for me with the same love and
patience
you show your orchids

to all my orchids
those who showed me that my sensitivity
is all the strength i need

to you
for blooming with me
only when we grow together
may we rise a garden

about the author

Kamilla Tolnø is a danish writer and dreamer.
her entire life has been led by her love for lan-
guage and the art of writing. apart from working
several years as a copywriter she has published a
danish short story collection in 2017.

she has created and shared minimalistic poetry
and illustrations on her social media channels for
years, reaching readers all across the globe.

the northern collection is her debut as an interna-
tionally renown poet. growing up amongst pine
trees and snowflakes inspired her to name this
collection after her place of origin.

apart from writing her soul burns for travel and
arts. and she wishes to experience it all with her
heart open and eyes closed.

more art on ktolnoe.com
or social media @k.tolnoe

the northern collection

the orchid is the second of four books in *the northern collection*. a manifestation of the internal journey that we must all face at some point in our lives; the journey to our true north. to our home.

the true north is a place that's different to everyone. it's the place where all the energetic lines meet. where we find answers and find peace. for we cannot help the world until we help ourselves.

the northern collection is most of all a place to unite. to grow. to heal. to become. together. i invite you to share any thoughts, feelings or dreams you may have with me. for us to come together as a community. and to serve as inspiration for the next books and steps to come.

join the conversation on ktolnoe.com or social media channels @k.tolnoe

Made in the USA
Las Vegas, NV
14 February 2021

17770211R00065